Contents

What Dots?

Sometimes we see things that are not true. Sometimes we see things that are not there. Our eyes play tricks on us. They see one thing, but our brains tell us it is something else.

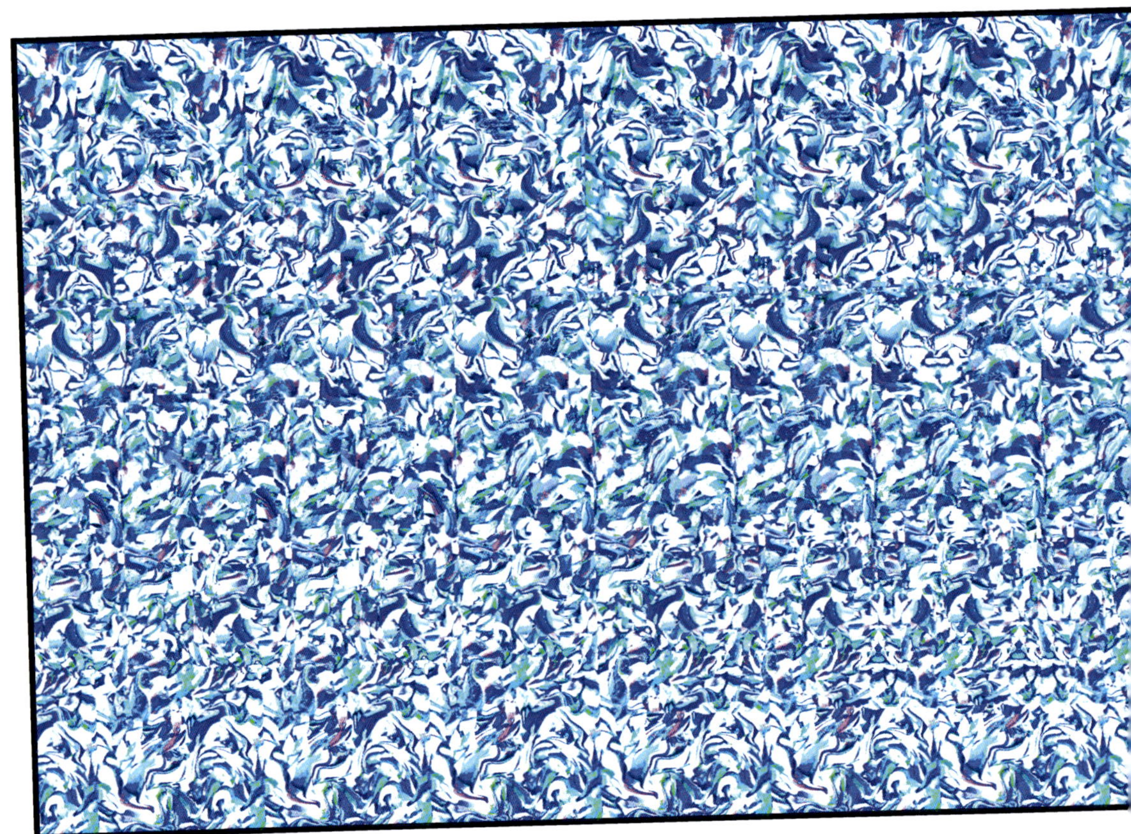

This is a Magic Eye picture. Stare into the picture. What can you see? Turn to page 24 to find out.

Look at this **pattern**.
Do you see some black dots?

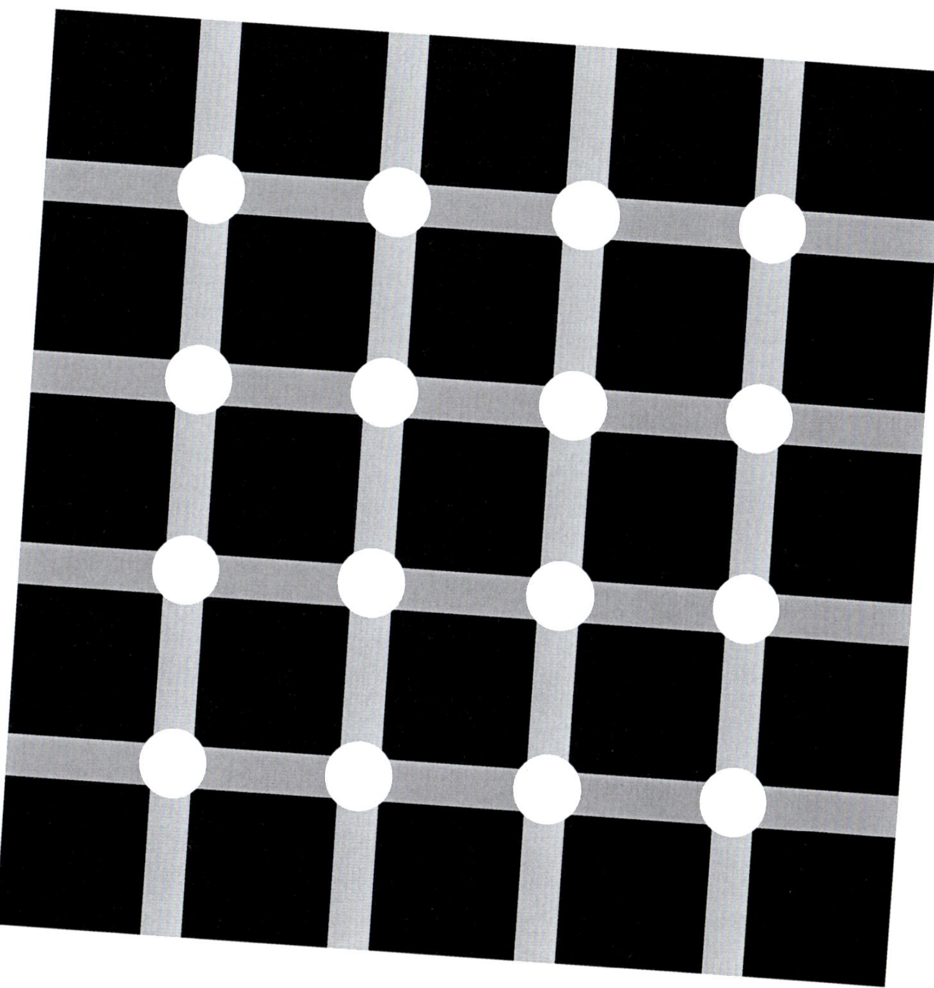

Look again. Can you count them?
Are the black dots really there at all?
This is an **optical illusion**.

Look at Lines

Now look at these lines.
Which line is the shortest?
Which line is the longest?

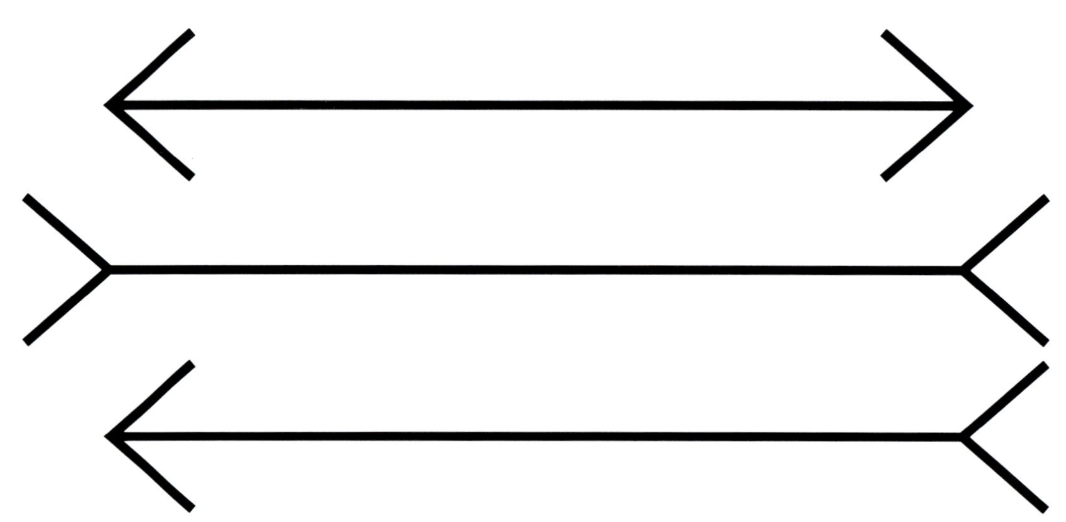

Look at the lines now.
They are all the same length.
Get a ruler and check!

Look at these rows of rectangles. Do the rows look bent?

Believe it or not, the rows are not bent. They just look bent because of the way the rectangles are placed.

This famous illusion is now a building!

Other buildings have optical illusions in them too. This is the floor of a shopping centre.

Move It!

Now try this.
Lie the book flat.
Look at the black dot
in the middle.
Move your head closer.
Move your head back.
What happens?

The shapes seem to move
because of the way they
are placed.

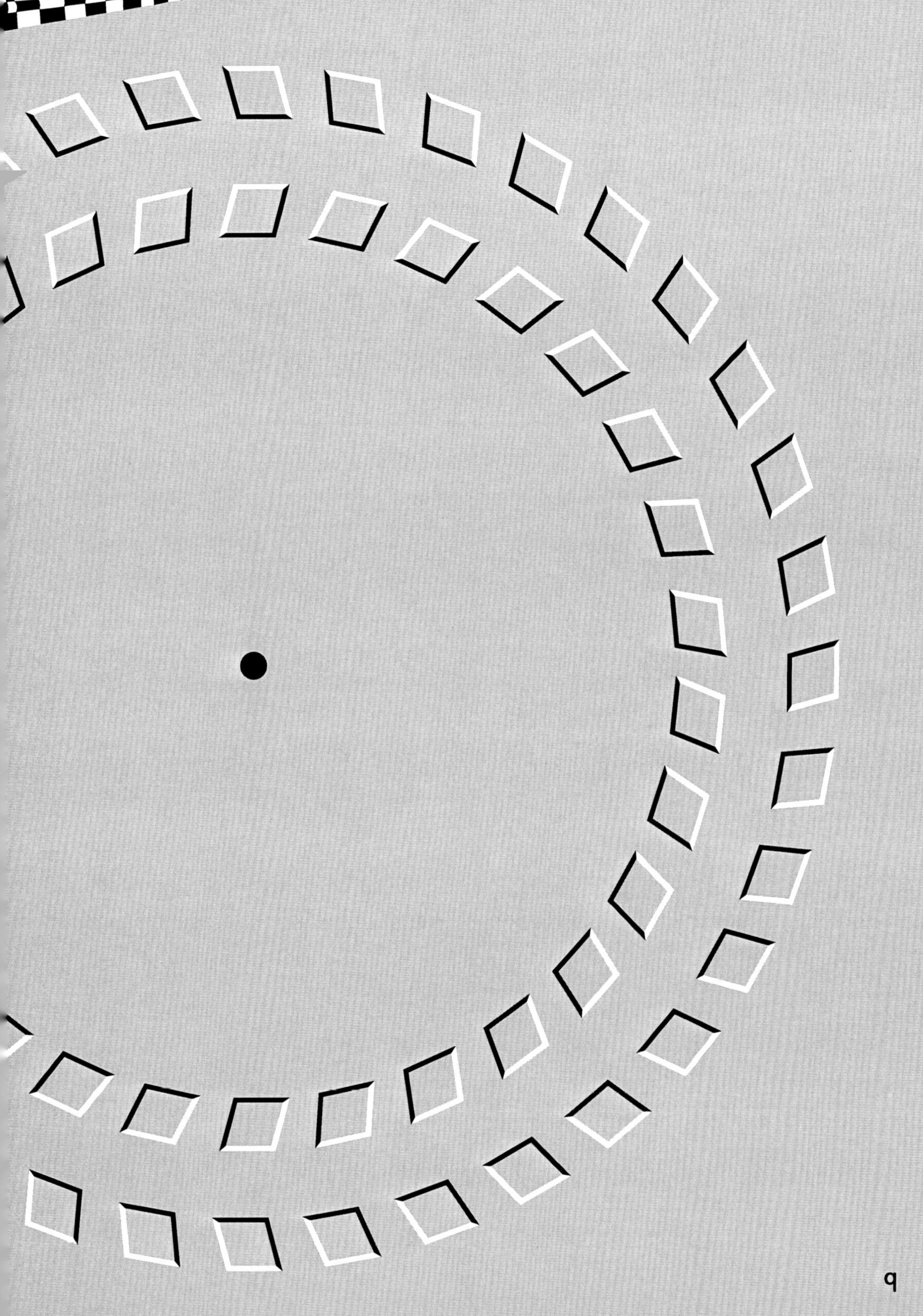

Look at this pattern of shapes and colours.

As our eyes move across the picture, the wheels seem to turn.

The patterns of colour make us think we can see wheels moving.

Fun with Words

There are optical illusions made with words too.

Do you see two words in this picture?
First look for one word.
Then look for a second word.

Now try this one.

Read from left to right.
Say the colour of each word.
Don't say the word!

red blue orange purple

orange blue green red

blue purple red green

orange blue orange red

purple orange red blue

green red blue purple

orange blue red green

purple orange red blue

Picture This

Sometimes, you need to look more than once at a picture to see what is in it.

Look at this picture.
What do you see in the white space?
What do you see in the black space?

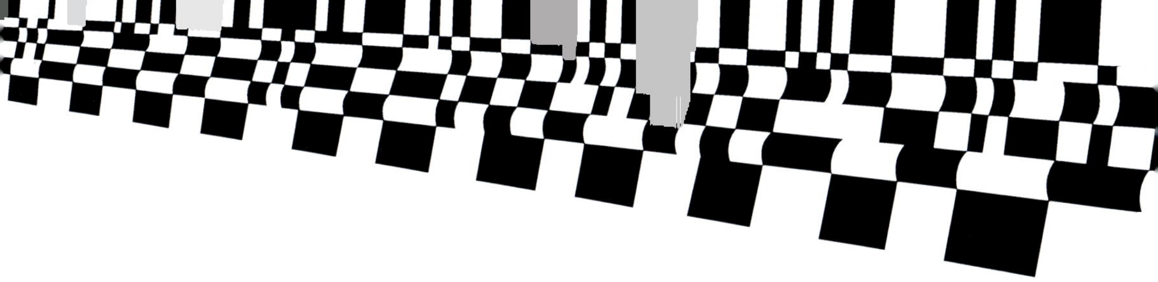

The white space shows a vase. The black space shows two heads looking at each other.

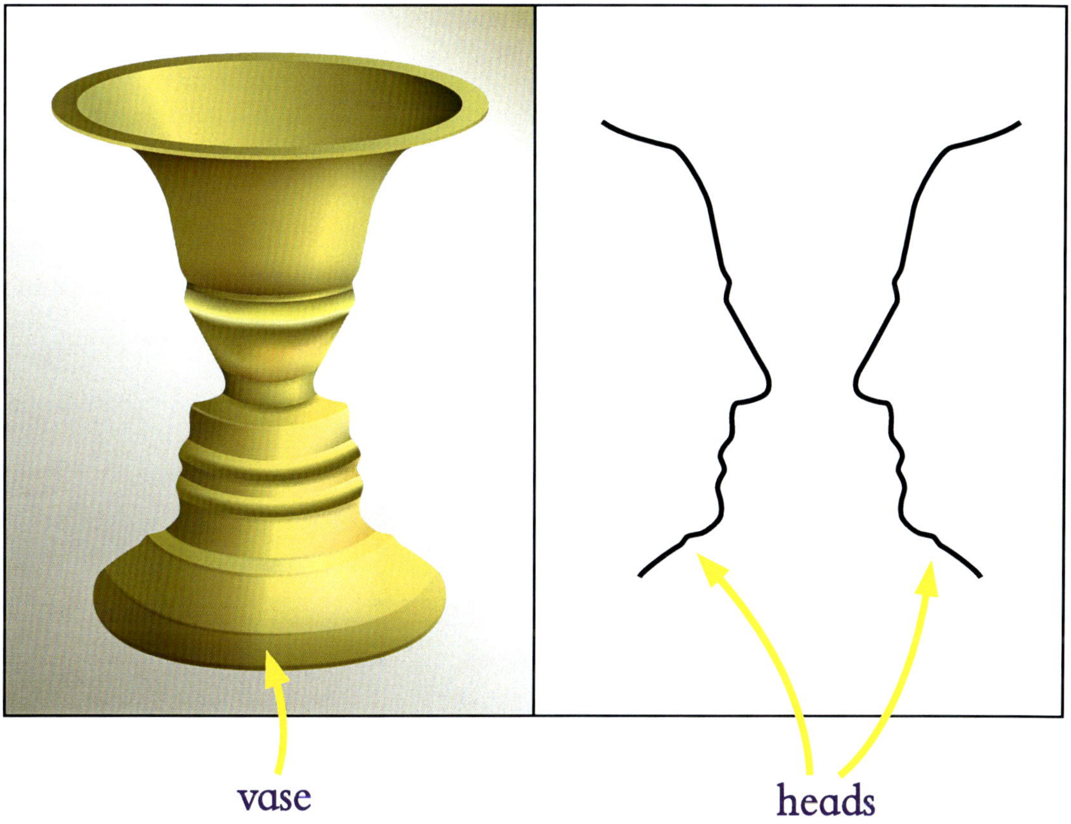

vase

heads

Like the vase illusion, this picture can **reveal** two different things. What do you see?

Do you see the young girl or the old woman? Can you see both?

This famous illusion first appeared on a German postcard in 1888.

Now look at these pictures.
Show a friend and talk about what you see.
Did you both see the same things?

Picture 1: a duck and a rabbit
Picture 2: a seal and a polar bear

Where Is It?

There are optical illusions in **nature** too. Many plants and animals use optical illusion for **camouflage**.

There is more to this photo than you first see! This photo shows a moth and leaves. Can you see the moth?

Here is the moth. Did you see it when you first looked at the picture?

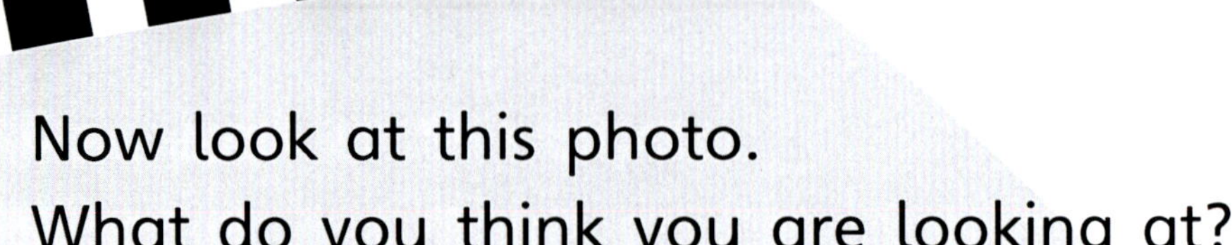

Now look at this photo.
What do you think you are looking at?

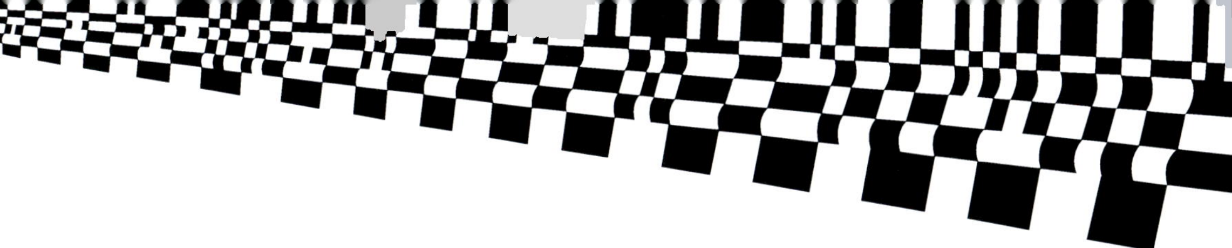

If you said “rocks”, you are only half right. You are also looking at plants.

These plants are called lithops, which means “like stone”. They blend in with the rocks around them to stop animals from eating them!

How Did They Do That?

Some artists play tricks in their art. They make us think we are looking at something that is real.

This amazing ice cliff is drawn with chalk.

This artist uses paint to camouflage himself. Can you see him?

Tricks of the Eye

Optical illusions are tricks of the eye and brain. What you see is not always as it seems ...

Glossary

camouflage	ways of blending in or becoming less visible
nature	the natural world, such as plants, animals, mountains
optical illusion	something we see that we think is real or true, but is not
pattern	things arranged in repeated ways
reveal	to show

Answer: page 2
Magic Eye picture